6l

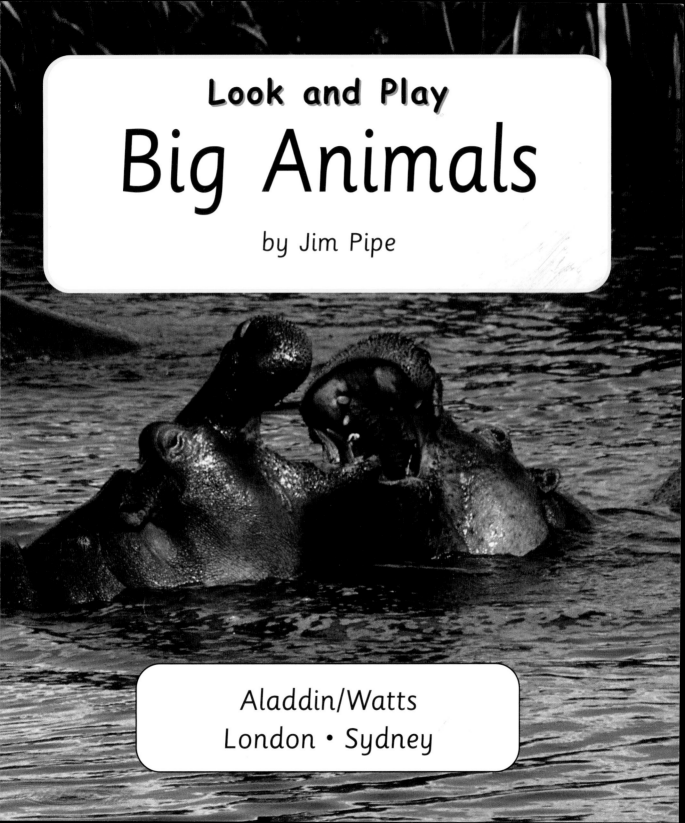

Look and Play
Big Animals

by Jim Pipe

Aladdin/Watts
London • Sydney

big

This bear is **big**.

3

camel

4

A **camel** is big, too.

5

eagle

An **eagle** is
a big bird.

shark

A **shark** is
a big fish.

9

bison

A **bison** is big and hairy.

giraffe

A **giraffe** is big and tall.

rhino

14

A **rhino** is
big and wide.

15

elephant

16

An **elephant** is bigger.

17

whale

18

A **whale** is the biggest.

19

Who am I?

rhino

elephant

giraffe

bear

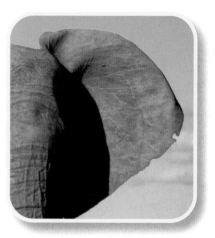

20 Match the words and pictures.

How many?

Can you count the elephants? **21**

Where am I?

Bear

Lion

Shark

Camel

Where do these big animals live?

Index

For Parents and Teachers

Questions you could ask:

p. 2 How big is a bear? Ask the reader to guess how big the animals in the book are, e.g. a bear is almost as big as a small car (up to 3.3 m long and 650kg).

p. 4 What big animals do people ride on? e.g. horses, camels, elephants. Point out the reins and saddle that help a rider to control/stay on the camel.

p. 6 What other big birds do you know? The biggest birds do not fly, e.g. ostrich, emu, but they can run very fast.

p. 8 What do sharks like to eat? Sharks eat fish and seals. But many other big animals are plant eaters: e.g. elephants, rhinos, giraffes, bison, camels.

p. 10 Can you see the bison's horns? Male bisons use their horns to fight each other. Ask readers if they know any other big animals with horns/antlers, e.g. reindeer, moose, buffalo, cattle, yak, rhinos.

p. 12 What is the longest part of a giraffe? A giraffe has a long neck to help it eat the leaves from the top of trees.

p. 16 Can you see its nose? An elephant's nose is called a trunk. It can smell, pick up and carry things, dig in the ground or spray water or dust.

p. 18 Can you see the diver (just below the whale's mouth)? The diver shows you just how big a whale is: it is 31 metres long (as long as 8 cars) and weighs 125 tonnes (the same as 1,670 people!)

Activities you could do:

• Go outside and ask readers to measure out how big the animals are, e.g. if one pace is 0.5 m, bear = 6-7 paces, elephant = 18 paces, whale = 62 paces!

• Role play: ask the reader to act out their favourite big animal, e.g. elephant swinging its trunk, giant eagle flapping its wings, rhino charging.

• Plan a day for children to bring a "big animal" stuffed toy to school (dinosaurs too!). Encourage them to share information about their animals.

• Ask children to count their toes. Elephants have 4 toes on their front feet, and 3 on the back feet!

© Aladdin Books Ltd 2007

Designed and produced by
Aladdin Books Ltd
2/3 Fitzroy Mews
London W1T 6DF

First published in 2007
in Great Britain
by Franklin Watts
338 Euston Road
London NW1 3BH

Franklin Watts Australia
Level 17/207 Kent Street
Sydney NSW 2000

Franklin Watts is a division of Hachette Children's Books.

ISBN 978 0 7496 7728 2

A catalogue record for this book is available from the British Library.

Dewey Classification: 590

Printed in Malaysia

Series consultant
Zoe Stillwell is an experienced Early Years teacher currently teaching at Pewley Down Infant School, Guildford.

Photocredits:
l-left, r-right, b-bottom, t-top, c-centre, m-middle
All photos on from istockphoto.com except: Cover, 1, 8-9, 14-15, 18-19, 20bl, 22bl & tr — Corbis. 6-7, 23mlb — Stockbyte. 10-11, 23mrt – US Fish and Wildlife Service. 23ml, tr, mrt & mrb — Ingram. 22bl — John Foxx.